W9-AUO-277

Today Is Great!

A DAILY
GRATITUDE JOURNAL
FOR KIDS

TODAY IS GREAT

By Vicky Perreault

ROCKRIDGE
PRESS

Copyright © 2019 by Rockridge Press, Emeryville, California

No part of this publication may be reproduced, stored in a retrieval system or transmitted in any form or by any means, electronic, mechanical, photocopying, recording, scanning or otherwise, except as permitted under Sections 107 or 108 of the 1976 United States Copyright Act, without the prior written permission of the Publisher. Requests to the Publisher for permission should be addressed to the Permissions Department, Rockridge Press, 6005 Shellmound Street, Suite 175, Emeryville, CA 94608.

Limit of Liability/Disclaimer of Warranty: The Publisher and the author make no representations or warranties with respect to the accuracy or completeness of the contents of this work and specifically disclaim all warranties, including without limitation warranties of fitness for a particular purpose. No warranty may be created or extended by sales or promotional materials. The advice and strategies contained herein may not be suitable for every situation. This work is sold with the understanding that the publisher is not engaged in rendering medical, legal, or other professional advice or services. If professional assistance is required, the services of a competent professional person should be sought. Neither the Publisher nor the author shall be liable for damages arising herefrom. The fact that an individual, organization or website is referred to in this work as a citation and/or potential source of further information does not mean that the author or the Publisher endorses the information the individual, organization or website may provide or recommendations they/it may make. Further, readers should be aware that Internet websites listed in this work may have changed or disappeared between when this work was written and when it is read.

For general information on our other products and services or to obtain technical support, please contact our Customer Care Department within the U.S. at (866) 744-2665, or outside the U.S. at (510) 253-0500.

Rockridge Press publishes its books in a variety of electronic and print formats. Some content that appears in print may not be available in electronic books, and vice versa.

TRADEMARKS: Rockridge Press and the Rockridge Press logo are trademarks or registered trademarks of Callisto Media Inc. and/or its affiliates, in the United States and other countries, and may not be used without written permission. All other trademarks are the property of their respective owners. Rockridge Press is not associated with any product or vendor mentioned in this book.

Interior and Cover Designer: Suzanne LaGasa
Photo Art Director: Sara Feinstein
Editor: Kristen Depken
Production Editor: Ashley Polikoff
Illustrations: © Revelstock Art/Creative Market; Studio Desset/Creative Market; Invisible Layer/Creative Market.
Author Photo Courtesy of © Bella Iranitalab.

ISBN: Print 978-1-64152-882-5

THIS BOOK BELONGS TO

_____.

YES!

INTRODUCTION

Have you ever felt gratitude before? Gratitude is noticing the good things in life and being thankful for them. One of the best ways to do this is by writing in a gratitude journal every day. Between school, homework, and activities, you may not always have time to notice the big and small moments of life. But even on the yuckiest of days, there is something to be grateful for, like a smile or a hug.

That's where this daily gratitude journal comes in. Every day, you'll have space to list the one thing you're most grateful for, such as seeing a rainbow or hanging out with a friend. You can use words, phrases, or sentences. How you write isn't important. What's important is that you get in the habit of writing. Try to write in your journal at the same time each day, maybe after school or before bed.

This journal also has weekly questions that will take more time. You can save those for the weekend. These questions will get you thinking about gratitude in a new way. Every other week, you'll get to take on a gratitude challenge. These are fun ways to promote kindness and spread gratitude. To keep you motivated, there are also positive quotes from some pretty smart people for you to read and share.

It takes just a few minutes a day to build your gratitude muscle. When you do, you'll start noticing more things to appreciate each day, and you may feel happier and more hopeful. Now **that** is something to write about!

Today I'm grateful for . . .

MONDAY		/ /
TUESDAY		/ /
WEDNESDAY		/ /
THURSDAY		/ /
FRIDAY		/ /
SATURDAY		/ /
SUNDAY		/ /

Name one special talent you have. How do you use it?

GRATITUDE CHALLENGE!

Write a thank you note to someone who has done something kind for you.

Today I'm grateful for . . .

MONDAY ___/___/___

TUESDAY ___/___/___

WEDNESDAY ___/___/___

THURSDAY ___/___/___

FRIDAY ___/___/___

SATURDAY ___/___/___

SUNDAY ___/___/___

What was the best part of your week? Describe it below.

"We must find time to stop and thank the people who make a difference in our lives."

—JOHN F. KENNEDY, PRESIDENT

Today I'm grateful for . . .

MONDAY ____ / ____ / ____

TUESDAY ____ / ____ / ____

WEDNESDAY ____ / ____ / ____

THURSDAY ____ / ____ / ____

FRIDAY ____ / ____ / ____

SATURDAY ____ / ____ / ____

SUNDAY ____ / ____ / ____

What are three nice things that people did for you this week? How did their actions make you feel?

GRATITUDE CHALLENGE!

Pick a spot in your room to hang a photo or drawing of the people you're grateful for.

Today I'm grateful for . . .

MONDAY ____ / ____ / ____

TUESDAY ____ / ____ / ____

WEDNESDAY ____ / ____ / ____

THURSDAY ____ / ____ / ____

FRIDAY ____ / ____ / ____

SATURDAY ____ / ____ / ____

SUNDAY ____ / ____ / ____

Where is your favorite place to go?
Draw a picture of it below.

"No act of kindness,
no matter how small,
is ever wasted."

—AESOP, STORYTELLER

Today I'm grateful for . . .

MONDAY ____/____/____

TUESDAY ____/____/____

WEDNESDAY ____/____/____

THURSDAY ____/____/____

FRIDAY ____/____/____

SATURDAY ____/____/____

SUNDAY ____/____/____

Who is your best friend? What do you love about him or her?

GRATITUDE CHALLENGE!

At your next meal, think about all the people who worked to bring you the food you're eating. Discuss it with your family or say a silent thanks to them for their work.

Today I'm grateful for . . .

MONDAY ____ / ____ / ____

TUESDAY ____ / ____ / ____

WEDNESDAY ____ / ____ / ____

THURSDAY ____ / ____ / ____

FRIDAY ____ / ____ / ____

SATURDAY ____ / ____ / ____

SUNDAY ____ / ____ / ____

What did you do to help someone this week? How did you feel afterward?

"If you have good thoughts they will shine out of your face like sunbeams and you will always look lovely."

—ROALD DAHL, AUTHOR

Today I'm grateful for . . .

MONDAY ____ / ____ / ____

TUESDAY ____ / ____ / ____

WEDNESDAY ____ / ____ / ____

THURSDAY ____ / ____ / ____

FRIDAY ____ / ____ / ____

SATURDAY ____ / ____ / ____

SUNDAY ____ / ____ / ____

What's your favorite pet? It could be yours or someone else's. Draw a picture of it below.

GRATITUDE CHALLENGE!

Do something nice for someone else, but don't tell them you did it. For example, you could make your brother or sister's bed, or put away the dishes without anyone noticing.

Today I'm grateful for . . .

MONDAY ____/____/____

TUESDAY ____/____/____

WEDNESDAY ____/____/____

THURSDAY ____/____/____

FRIDAY ____/____/____

SATURDAY ____/____/____

SUNDAY ____/____/____

What is your favorite memory? Describe it below.

"If you see someone without a smile, give them one of yours."

—DOLLY PARTON, SINGER

Today I'm grateful for . . .

MONDAY ___/___/___

TUESDAY ___/___/___

WEDNESDAY ___/___/___

THURSDAY ___/___/___

FRIDAY ___/___/___

SATURDAY ___/___/___

SUNDAY ___/___/___

What is something you are really looking forward to? Why are you so excited about it?

GRATITUDE CHALLENGE!

Hold the door open for someone who has their hands full.

Today I'm grateful for . . .

MONDAY ____/____/____

TUESDAY ____/____/____

WEDNESDAY ____/____/____

THURSDAY ____/____/____

FRIDAY ____/____/____

SATURDAY ____/____/____

SUNDAY ____/____/____

What do you like best about yourself? Why?

"Folks are usually about as happy as they make their minds up to be."

—ABRAHAM LINCOLN, PRESIDENT

Today I'm grateful for . . .

MONDAY ____/____/____

TUESDAY ____/____/____

WEDNESDAY ____/____/____

THURSDAY ____/____/____

FRIDAY ____/____/____

SATURDAY ____/____/____

SUNDAY ____/____/____

What is your favorite book? Why do you love it?

GRATITUDE CHALLENGE!

Thank someone for something specific. For example, you could thank a friend for helping you with a math problem or a parent for making you lunch.

Today I'm grateful for . . .

MONDAY ___/___/___

TUESDAY ___/___/___

WEDNESDAY ___/___/___

THURSDAY ___/___/___

FRIDAY ___/___/___

SATURDAY ___/___/___

SUNDAY ___/___/___

What is your favorite spot in your house? What do you like to do there?

"Good words are worth much, and cost little."

—GEORGE HERBERT, POET

Today I'm grateful for . . .

MONDAY ____/____/____

TUESDAY ____/____/____

WEDNESDAY ____/____/____

THURSDAY ____/____/____

FRIDAY ____/____/____

SATURDAY ____/____/____

SUNDAY ____/____/____

Who is the funniest person you know?
What do they do that makes you laugh?

GRATITUDE CHALLENGE!

Say hello to someone in your school who you have never talked to before.

Today I'm grateful for . . .

MONDAY		/ /
TUESDAY		/ /
WEDNESDAY		/ /
THURSDAY		/ /
FRIDAY		/ /
SATURDAY		/ /
SUNDAY		/ /

What is one thing in nature that inspires you? Draw it below.

"Learn from yesterday, live for today, hope for tomorrow. The important thing is not to stop questioning."

—ALBERT EINSTEIN, PHYSICIST

Today I'm grateful for . . .

MONDAY ____ / ____ / ____

TUESDAY ____ / ____ / ____

WEDNESDAY ____ / ____ / ____

THURSDAY ____ / ____ / ____

FRIDAY ____ / ____ / ____

SATURDAY ____ / ____ / ____

SUNDAY ____ / ____ / ____

What is something new you learned this week? How will it help you?

GRATITUDE CHALLENGE!

Go through toys that you have outgrown and pick five to give to a younger brother, sister, or friend.

Today I'm grateful for . . .

MONDAY ____ / ____ / ____

TUESDAY ____ / ____ / ____

WEDNESDAY ____ / ____ / ____

THURSDAY ____ / ____ / ____

FRIDAY ____ / ____ / ____

SATURDAY ____ / ____ / ____

SUNDAY ____ / ____ / ____

Who are you most grateful for? Who do you think is most grateful for you?

"Life is short, but there is always time for courtesy."

—RALPH WALDO EMERSON, AUTHOR

Today I'm grateful for . . .

MONDAY ____/____/____

TUESDAY ____/____/____

WEDNESDAY ____/____/____

THURSDAY ____/____/____

FRIDAY ____/____/____

SATURDAY ____/____/____

SUNDAY ____/____/____

If you could have your favorite meal for dinner, what would it be? What would you have for dessert?

GRATITUDE CHALLENGE!

Write a thank you note to the person who delivers your mail. Leave it in your mailbox for them.

Today I'm grateful for . . .

MONDAY ____ / ____ / ____

TUESDAY ____ / ____ / ____

WEDNESDAY ____ / ____ / ____

THURSDAY ____ / ____ / ____

FRIDAY ____ / ____ / ____

SATURDAY ____ / ____ / ____

SUNDAY ____ / ____ / ____

What is the best vacation you've ever been on? What did you love about it?

"When we give cheerfully and accept gratefully, everyone is blessed."

—MAYA ANGELOU, POET

Today I'm grateful for . . .

MONDAY	/ /
TUESDAY	/ /
WEDNESDAY	/ /
THURSDAY	/ /
FRIDAY	/ /
SATURDAY	/ /
SUNDAY	/ /

Draw a self-portrait in the space below. Use a mirror to help you see what you look like.

GRATITUDE CHALLENGE!

Thank the person who does your laundry and offer to help them with it this week.

Today I'm grateful for . . .

MONDAY ___/___/___

TUESDAY ___/___/___

WEDNESDAY ___/___/___

THURSDAY ___/___/___

FRIDAY ___/___/___

SATURDAY ___/___/___

SUNDAY ___/___/___

What is your favorite song? How does it make you feel?

"The way to develop the best that is in a person is by appreciation and encouragement."

—CHARLES SCHWAB, INVESTOR

Today I'm grateful for . . .

MONDAY ____/____/____

TUESDAY ____/____/____

WEDNESDAY ____/____/____

THURSDAY ____/____/____

FRIDAY ____/____/____

SATURDAY ____/____/____

SUNDAY ____/____/____

Describe your perfect day. Who would you spend it with? What would you do?

GRATITUDE CHALLENGE!

Write a positive message in sidewalk chalk somewhere a lot of people will see it. For example: "You are special." or "Believe in yourself." or "You are brave."

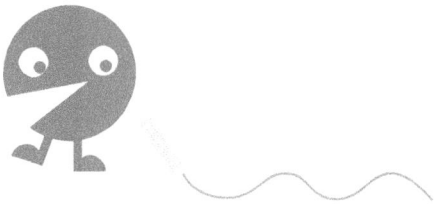

Today I'm grateful for . . .

MONDAY ___/___/___

TUESDAY ___/___/___

WEDNESDAY ___/___/___

THURSDAY ___/___/___

FRIDAY ___/___/___

SATURDAY ___/___/___

SUNDAY ___/___/___

What do you like best about the way you look? What do you think is the first thing people notice about you?

"Do not let what you cannot do interfere with what you can do."

—JOHN WOODEN, BASKETBALL COACH

Today I'm grateful for . . .

MONDAY ____ / ____ / ____

TUESDAY ____ / ____ / ____

WEDNESDAY ____ / ____ / ____

THURSDAY ____ / ____ / ____

FRIDAY ____ / ____ / ____

SATURDAY ____ / ____ / ____

SUNDAY ____ / ____ / ____

Who do you like to talk to when you need help with something? Who is best at cheering you up?

GRATITUDE CHALLENGE!

Count the number of people who smile at you in one day.

Today I'm grateful for . . .

MONDAY ___/___/___

TUESDAY ___/___/___

WEDNESDAY ___/___/___

THURSDAY ___/___/___

FRIDAY ___/___/___

SATURDAY ___/___/___

SUNDAY ___/___/___

What is your favorite family tradition? Describe it below.

"Winning doesn't always mean being first. Winning means you're doing better than you've done before."

—BONNIE BLAIR, AMERICAN SPEED SKATER

Today I'm grateful for . . .

MONDAY ____ / ____ / ____

TUESDAY ____ / ____ / ____

WEDNESDAY ____ / ____ / ____

THURSDAY ____ / ____ / ____

FRIDAY ____ / ____ / ____

SATURDAY ____ / ____ / ____

SUNDAY ____ / ____ / ____

Who said something nice to you this week? What did they say? How did it make you feel?

GRATITUDE CHALLENGE!

When you finish reading a book, leave it in a public place, like on a park bench or a bus, for someone else to find. Include a note that says you are passing the book on for someone else to enjoy.

Today I'm grateful for . . .

MONDAY ___/___/___

TUESDAY ___/___/___

WEDNESDAY ___/___/___

THURSDAY ___/___/___

FRIDAY ___/___/___

SATURDAY ___/___/___

SUNDAY ___/___/___

Describe an act of kindness you witnessed this week.

"In any moment of decision, the best thing you can do is the right thing. The worst thing you can do is nothing."

—THEODORE ROOSEVELT, PRESIDENT

Today I'm grateful for . . .

MONDAY ___/___/___

TUESDAY ___/___/___

WEDNESDAY ___/___/___

THURSDAY ___/___/___

FRIDAY ___/___/___

SATURDAY ___/___/___

SUNDAY ___/___/___

What is your favorite thing about each season?

WINTER:

SPRING:

SUMMER:

FALL:

GRATITUDE CHALLENGE!

Offer to clear the table after dinner one night this week.

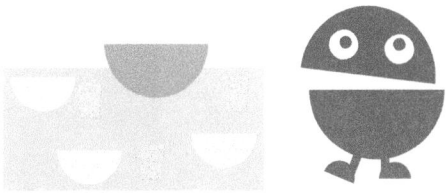

Today I'm grateful for . . .

MONDAY ____/____/____

TUESDAY ____/____/____

WEDNESDAY ____/____/____

THURSDAY ____/____/____

FRIDAY ____/____/____

SATURDAY ____/____/____

SUNDAY ____/____/____

What is your favorite thing to do outside? Describe it below.

"Yesterday is history. Tomorrow is a mystery. Today is a gift. That's why we call it 'The Present.'"

—ELEANOR ROOSEVELT, FIRST LADY

Today I'm grateful for . . .

MONDAY ____ / ____ / ____

TUESDAY ____ / ____ / ____

WEDNESDAY ____ / ____ / ____

THURSDAY ____ / ____ / ____

FRIDAY ____ / ____ / ____

SATURDAY ____ / ____ / ____

SUNDAY ____ / ____ / ____

Describe your family. What makes it special?

GRATITUDE CHALLENGE!

Do something nice for a teacher, like drawing them a picture, bringing in a treat, or offering to help with something in their classroom.

Today I'm grateful for . . .

MONDAY ___/___/___

TUESDAY ___/___/___

WEDNESDAY ___/___/___

THURSDAY ___/___/___

FRIDAY ___/___/___

SATURDAY ___/___/___

SUNDAY ___/___/___

What are five words your friends would use to describe you?

"Be silly. Be honest. Be kind."

—RALPH WALDO EMERSON, AUTHOR

Today I'm grateful for . . .

MONDAY ____ / ____ / ____

TUESDAY ____ / ____ / ____

WEDNESDAY ____ / ____ / ____

THURSDAY ____ / ____ / ____

FRIDAY ____ / ____ / ____

SATURDAY ____ / ____ / ____

SUNDAY ____ / ____ / ____

What is your favorite sport to play? What is your favorite sport to watch? Why do you like them?

GRATITUDE CHALLENGE!

Look for a classmate who is eating lunch alone, and invite them to join you.

Today I'm grateful for . . .

MONDAY ____/____/____

TUESDAY ____/____/____

WEDNESDAY ____/____/____

THURSDAY ____/____/____

FRIDAY ____/____/____

SATURDAY ____/____/____

SUNDAY ____/____/____

What three things that you own do you value the most?

"Without the rain,
there would be no rainbow."

—G.K. CHESTERTON, AUTHOR

Today I'm grateful for . . .

MONDAY ___/___/___

TUESDAY ___/___/___

WEDNESDAY ___/___/___

THURSDAY ___/___/___

FRIDAY ___/___/___

SATURDAY ___/___/___

SUNDAY ___/___/___

What is your favorite smell? When and where do you usually smell it?

GRATITUDE CHALLENGE!

Write some positive messages on sticky notes and stick them up around the house where your family will see them. You can write things like "You're the best!" and "I love you!"

Today I'm grateful for . . .

MONDAY ___/___/___

TUESDAY ___/___/___

WEDNESDAY ___/___/___

THURSDAY ___/___/___

FRIDAY ___/___/___

SATURDAY ___/___/___

SUNDAY ___/___/___

Describe a time when someone helped you solve a problem. Who was it? How did they help you?

"Be thankful for what you have; you'll end up having more. If you concentrate on what you don't have, you will never, ever have enough."

—OPRAH WINFREY, MEDIA EXECUTIVE

Today I'm grateful for . . .

MONDAY ____/____/____

TUESDAY ____/____/____

WEDNESDAY ____/____/____

THURSDAY ____/____/____

FRIDAY ____/____/____

SATURDAY ____/____/____

SUNDAY ____/____/____

Describe a time when someone surprised you with kindness. What did they do, and how did it make you feel?

GRATITUDE CHALLENGE!

Tell a family member or friend what you like about them.

Today I'm grateful for . . .

MONDAY ___/___/___

TUESDAY ___/___/___

WEDNESDAY ___/___/___

THURSDAY ___/___/___

FRIDAY ___/___/___

SATURDAY ___/___/___

SUNDAY ___/___/___

Which of your five senses (sight, hearing, touch, taste, smell) are you the most grateful for? Why?

"Carry out a random act of kindness, with no expectation of reward, safe in the knowledge that one day someone might do the same for you."

—DIANA, PRINCESS OF WALES

Today I'm grateful for . . .

MONDAY ____ / ____ / ____

TUESDAY ____ / ____ / ____

WEDNESDAY ____ / ____ / ____

THURSDAY ____ / ____ / ____

FRIDAY ____ / ____ / ____

SATURDAY ____ / ____ / ____

SUNDAY ____ / ____ / ____

What was the best birthday you've ever had? Why was it so great?

GRATITUDE CHALLENGE!

Ask an adult to take you to a local park. Bring a garbage bag and gloves, and pick up any trash you find there.

Today I'm grateful for . . .

MONDAY ___/___/___

TUESDAY ___/___/___

WEDNESDAY ___/___/___

THURSDAY ___/___/___

FRIDAY ___/___/___

SATURDAY ___/___/___

SUNDAY ___/___/___

Pick one family member. It could be a parent, sibling, grandparent, or other relative. How does he or she make your life better?

"The time is always right to do what is right."

—MARTIN LUTHER KING JR., MINISTER AND ACTIVIST

Today I'm grateful for . . .

MONDAY ____ / ____ / ____

TUESDAY ____ / ____ / ____

WEDNESDAY ____ / ____ / ____

THURSDAY ____ / ____ / ____

FRIDAY ____ / ____ / ____

SATURDAY ____ / ____ / ____

SUNDAY ____ / ____ / ____

What is your favorite holiday? What do you do to celebrate it?

GRATITUDE CHALLENGE!

With an adult's help, bake brownies and hand them out to your neighbors.

Today I'm grateful for . . .

MONDAY ____/____/____

TUESDAY ____/____/____

WEDNESDAY ____/____/____

THURSDAY ____/____/____

FRIDAY ____/____/____

SATURDAY ____/____/____

SUNDAY ____/____/____

What teacher has made the biggest difference in your life? What did they do that was so special?

"Friendship is born at that moment when one person says to another, 'What! You too? I thought I was the only one.'"

—C. S. LEWIS, WRITER

Today I'm grateful for . . .

MONDAY ___/___/___

TUESDAY ___/___/___

WEDNESDAY ___/___/___

THURSDAY ___/___/___

FRIDAY ___/___/___

SATURDAY ___/___/___

SUNDAY ___/___/___

What was the most delicious thing you ate this week? Who made it for you? What made it so good?

GRATITUDE CHALLENGE!

Compliment three people on something they have done well.

Today I'm grateful for . . .

MONDAY ___/___/___

TUESDAY ___/___/___

WEDNESDAY ___/___/___

THURSDAY ___/___/___

FRIDAY ___/___/___

SATURDAY ___/___/___

SUNDAY ___/___/___

What subject in school do you enjoy most? What do you like about it?

"The only way to have a friend is to be one."

—RALPH WALDO EMERSON, AUTHOR

Today I'm grateful for . . .

MONDAY ____ / ____ / ____

TUESDAY ____ / ____ / ____

WEDNESDAY ____ / ____ / ____

THURSDAY ____ / ____ / ____

FRIDAY ____ / ____ / ____

SATURDAY ____ / ____ / ____

SUNDAY ____ / ____ / ____

When was the last time you said "I love you"? Who did you say it to?

GRATITUDE CHALLENGE!

Offer to help someone in class who is struggling with a subject you're good at.

Today I'm grateful for . . .

MONDAY ___/___/___

TUESDAY ___/___/___

WEDNESDAY ___/___/___

THURSDAY ___/___/___

FRIDAY ___/___/___

SATURDAY ___/___/___

SUNDAY ___/___/___

What was the best gift you have ever received? Was it something you had wanted for a long time or a surprise that you ended up loving?

"The more you like yourself, the less you are like anyone else, which makes you unique."

—WALT DISNEY, ANIMATOR

Today I'm grateful for . . .

MONDAY	/ /
TUESDAY	/ /
WEDNESDAY	/ /
THURSDAY	/ /
FRIDAY	/ /
SATURDAY	/ /
SUNDAY	/ /

What can you do to brighten someone's day tomorrow?

GRATITUDE CHALLENGE!

Invite a new friend to hang out with you. This could be someone in your class that you don't know very well or someone who just moved to your neighborhood.

Today I'm grateful for . . .

MONDAY ___/___/___

TUESDAY ___/___/___

WEDNESDAY ___/___/___

THURSDAY ___/___/___

FRIDAY ___/___/___

SATURDAY ___/___/___

SUNDAY ___/___/___

Describe a time when you were brave. What did you do? Was it easy or hard?

"We do not need magic to transform the world. We carry all the power we need inside ourselves already. We have the power to imagine better."

—J. K. ROWLING, WRITER

Today I'm grateful for . . .

MONDAY ____/____/____

TUESDAY ____/____/____

WEDNESDAY ____/____/____

THURSDAY ____/____/____

FRIDAY ____/____/____

SATURDAY ____/____/____

SUNDAY ____/____/____

What time of day do you like best: mornings, afternoons, or evenings? What do you like to do during that time?

GRATITUDE CHALLENGE!

Ask a grandparent or older relative what they liked to do for fun when they were your age.

Today I'm grateful for . . .

MONDAY ___/___/___

TUESDAY ___/___/___

WEDNESDAY ___/___/___

THURSDAY ___/___/___

FRIDAY ___/___/___

SATURDAY ___/___/___

SUNDAY ___/___/___

What is your favorite way to exercise? For example, it could be running, dancing, or playing soccer.

"Kind words can be short and easy to speak, but their echoes are truly endless."

—MOTHER TERESA, HUMANITARIAN

Today I'm grateful for . . .

MONDAY ____ / ____ / ____

TUESDAY ____ / ____ / ____

WEDNESDAY ____ / ____ / ____

THURSDAY ____ / ____ / ____

FRIDAY ____ / ____ / ____

SATURDAY ____ / ____ / ____

SUNDAY ____ / ____ / ____

What made you laugh this week? Why was it so funny?

GRATITUDE CHALLENGE!

Tell three people your favorite joke.

Today I'm grateful for . . .

MONDAY ___/___/___

TUESDAY ___/___/___

WEDNESDAY ___/___/___

THURSDAY ___/___/___

FRIDAY ___/___/___

SATURDAY ___/___/___

SUNDAY ___/___/___

What is your favorite hobby? What do you like about it?

"When I started counting my blessings, my whole life turned around."

—WILLIE NELSON, MUSICIAN

Today I'm grateful for . . .

MONDAY	/ /
TUESDAY	/ /
WEDNESDAY	/ /
THURSDAY	/ /
FRIDAY	/ /
SATURDAY	/ /
SUNDAY	/ /

What do you love the most about your life?

GRATITUDE CHALLENGE!

With an adult's help, collect food to donate to a local soup kitchen or shelter.

Today I'm grateful for . . .

MONDAY ____ / ____ / ____

TUESDAY ____ / ____ / ____

WEDNESDAY ____ / ____ / ____

THURSDAY ____ / ____ / ____

FRIDAY ____ / ____ / ____

SATURDAY ____ / ____ / ____

SUNDAY ____ / ____ / ____

What do you like most about keeping a gratitude journal? How has it helped you?

"It always seems impossible until it is done."

—NELSON MANDELA, POLITICAL LEADER

ABOUT THE AUTHOR

Vicky Perreault is the founder of *Mess for Less* (www.messforless.net) where she shares kids' activities, parenting tips, and family-friendly recipes. She is a former teacher who holds a master's degree in early childhood and elementary education. She uses that experience to create fun learning opportunities for her children and her blog readers. Vicky is the mom of three amazing girls and the wife of the best husband anyone could ask for. She is grateful for them all.

CPSIA information can be obtained
at www.ICGtesting.com
Printed in the USA
JSHW011509171120
9654JS00005B/30

9 781641 528825